THE LITTLE BOOK OF

HORRORS

Published in 2022 by OH!
An Imprint of Welbeck Non-Fiction Limited,
part of Welbeck Publishing Group.
Based in London and Sydney.
www.welbeckpublishing.com

Compilation text © Welbeck Non-Fiction Limited 2022
Design © Welbeck Non-Fiction Limited 2022

ISBN 978-1-80069-235-0

Compiled and written by: Malcolm Croft
Editorial: Victoria Denne
Project manager: Russell Porter
Production: Jess Brisley

A CIP catalogue record for this book is available from the British Library

Printed in China

10 9 8 7 6 5 4 3 2 1

Images: Shutterstock.com

THE LITTLE BOOK OF
HORRORS

SPOOKY WIT & WISDOM
FOR HALLOWEEN AND BEYOND

CONTENTS

INTRODUCTION – 6

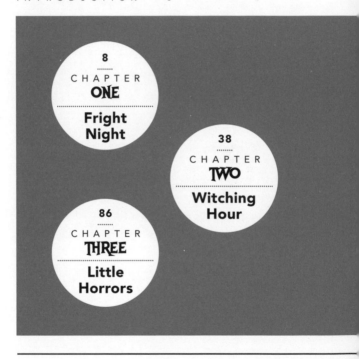

8

CHAPTER
ONE

**Fright
Night**

38

CHAPTER
TWO

**Witching
Hour**

86

CHAPTER
THREE

**Little
Horrors**

126

CHAPTER
FOUR

Smashing Pumpkins

158

CHAPTER
FIVE

Terror Vision

174

CHAPTER
SIX

Hell Raisers

TRICK OR TREAT?

Welcome to the stuff of nightmares. In fun-size book form. Yes, this tiny tome is your ideal coffin companion, a delicious snack to keep the grouchy monsters under your bed trick-and-treated for hours; a ghoulishly grisly (and giddy) guide to everything that's great about things that are generally quite horrible.

For more than two millennia, humankind has scared itself silly celebrating all things spooky, supernatural and sinister within the confines of this odd-numbered date. In a parodic twist of paradox irony, the nightmares of the real world have become more terrifying than the imagined horrors we faux-fear of Halloween, with the evening remaining the one highlight of the year where we can actually relax into the relative safety net of collectively suspended disbelief, and dive deep into the macabre underworld of what lies beneath without incurring actual GBH. While browsing this realm, our families and friends can play dead in that slithery sliver of twilight between the spirit dominion and ours… and open a portal to another devilish domain.

At the time of writing, Halloween remains more important – and even bigger business – than ever before. It's a multi-billion buck-raker that caters to every soul that walks the boundary between life, death and consumerism. As an annual cash cow, the horror industry of Halloweening feeds on popular culture trends – a polter-zeitgeist, if you will – remaining relevant, swelling with size every *annus horribilis*. After 2,000 years, Halloween has yet to get old. And it never will. Unlike Christmas, which is a total snooze-fest these days.

Using a bit of black magic, witches' brew and dash of ectoplasm, trick-or-treating transforms adults into kids, children into heroes, and parents into party animals; it's truly an event that caters to the kids of all ages, and wickedly wholesome fun for the whole family.

This *Little Book of Horrors* is an all-thriller no-filler horror show. Full of freaky facts, wicked wisecracks and sickening stats. Hell, the book itself will even make a great treat, fitting splendidly into any trick-or-treat bucket or pillowcase. Just a thought for next year.

Wait. What's that noise?

Something wicked this way comes. Are you afraid? You should be.

CHAPTER
ONE

FRIGHT NIGHT

Welcome to Hell. Don't even try to escape. And don't you dare put this book down either. If you do, you'll be cursed by a good witch friend of mine for all eternity. She does great cursing. Yes, Fright Night is upon us. Your spider senses are about to get all tingly with buckets of blood, sweat and fear. It's about to get full-on freaky in here. Let's go horror hunting...

HORRIPILATION

The rather perfect
word that describes the
sensation you feel
when – through fear,
excitement or chill – the
hairs stand up on the
back of your neck.

"
It's Halloween; everyone's entitled to one good scare.
"

Brackett
Halloween, (1978)

Every Halloween, most horror lovers throw their nutritious pumpkin seeds away and, somewhat ironically, fill their pumpkins with sugary candy. Pumpkin seeds are, however, a delicious superfood.

They are an incredible source of unsaturated fats, rich in antioxidants, great for blood-sugar balance, and can help prevent some cancers and cardiovascular disease.

They may be a trick for kids – but, for adults, they're a nutritional treat.

"

The greatest
trick the Devil
ever pulled
was convincing
the world he
didn't exist.

"

Keyser Söze
The Usual Suspects (1995)

THRILLER NIGHT

The final single from the world's bestselling album of the same name, "Thriller", was originally considered not worthy of release. "Who wants a single about monsters?", Walter Yetnikoff, executive of Michael Jackson's record label, infamously said of the song. MJ disagreed. The now-iconic music video, with its undead dancing, was first broadcast on Halloween 1983 and is described by the Library of Congress as "the most famous music video of all time".

For "Thriller", Vincent Price's
masterful macabre monologue
was written by the song's composer,
Rod Temperton, in a taxi on the
way to the studio and recorded
by Price in just two takes.

Easiest $20,000 he ever made.

HORROR

PLAYLIST#1

BAND NAMES

1. "Jellybelly" – **Smashing Pumpkins**

2. "Dragula" – **Rob Zombie**

3. "Bones" – **The Killers**

4. "I Can't Go To Sleep" – **Ghostface**

5. "Unbelievers" – **Vampire Weekend**

6. "Friend of the Devil" – **Grateful Dead**

7. "Black Magic" – **Slayer**

8. "The Ghost Within" – **And You Will Know Us By The Trail of Dead**

9. "Oblivion" – **Terrorvision**

10. "Down with the Clown" – **Insane Clown Posse**

TOP 10

HALLOWEEN CANDIES

According to Forbes in 2021 the US has
the sweetest of teeth for these sweet
treats, in terms of volume sold.

1. REESE'S CUPS
2. SKITTLES
3. M&MS
4. STARBURST
5. HOT TAMALES
6. SOUR PATCH KIDS
7. HERSHEY KISSES
8. SNICKERS
9. TOOTSIE POPS
10. CANDY CORN

17

Spread across 90,000 acres in six pumpkin-producing states – Illinois, Michigan, New York, Ohio, Pennsylvania and California – around 1.85 billion lbs of pumpkins were produced in the US in 2021.

A typical pumpkin weighs 13 lbs.

Today, the word **"bugbear"** is often used to describe a pet peeve.

Historically, the word was used to name a legendary bear creature that frightened children, emerging from the word **"bugaboo"**.

Deriving from the Middle English word **"bugge"** (to frighten), the root of **Boogeyman** and **"bogglins"** (**hobgoblins**), came from **bugbear**.

Would a pumpkin by any other name smell as sweet? Try these out for size...

1. *Jättiläiskurpitsa* – Finnish
2. *Potiron* – French
3. *Kürbis* – German
4. *Pepon* – Greek
5. *Popone* – Italian
6. *Kabocha* – Japanese
7. *Muskatgraskar* – Norwegian
8. *Calabaza* – Spanish
9. *Bisampumpa* – Swedish
10. *Graeske* – Danish

IN 2021,
HALLOWEENERS
IN THE UNITED
STATES SPENT
ON AVERAGE
$35 DOLLARS
PER PERSON
ON CANDY AND
COSTUMES.

MOST HAUNTED
#1
UNITED STATES

According to Forbes, these are the scariest, spookiest and most sinister US states.

1. Texas
(Most haunted spot: Driskill Hotel, Austin)

2. California
(Most haunted spot: Hollywood's Hotel Roosevelt)

3. Ohio
(Most haunted spot: Ohio State Reformatory, the location of *Shawshank* prison)

4. Michigan
(Most haunted spot: Mackinac Island's Grand Hotel, the world's longest porch)

5. Illinois
(Most haunted spot: Chicago's Congress Plaza Hotel; Al Capone is a regular haunt)

6. Indiana
(Most haunted spot: French Lick Springs Hotel)

7. Pennsylvania
(Most haunted spot: Gettysburg Hotel; haunted by a civil war nurse)

8. Oklahoma
(Most haunted spot: Blue Bell hotel, Guthrie)

9. New York
(Most haunted spot: everywhere, it's New York)

10. Virginia
(Most haunted spot: Black Horse Inn, Hunt Country)

In 2021, one in ten adults inthe US coordinated their costumes with another Halloweener.

It was the Roman statesman Pliny the Younger, in the first century AD, who recorded one of the first ghost stories.

Pliny reported that the spectre of an elderly man with a long beard, rattling chains, was haunting his house in Athens, Greece.

58%

of Americans
believe that places
can be haunted
by spirits.

PAREIDOLIA

(pronounced: "Pear-eye-doh-lee-ah")

If you've ever seen a face, or a body, or a familiar shape or pattern, in something that isn't actually there, you've been duped by Pareidolia. Put simply: this is where your brain fills in the gaps in what your eyes perceive.

27

RULES OF HALLOWEEN

1. Don't trick-a-treat a house that doesn't have inviting Halloween decorations outside.

2. Don't count your sweets until you get home.

3. Never trick a house after a treat.

4. Never take more than one treat (unless specifically invited to do so).

5. Leave a treat if a treat box is empty (for someone else).

6. Always say thank you (in your best monster voice).

7. Never complain about the quality of a treat (a treat's a treat).

8. Never go to the same house more than once (no matter how big the score).

9. Don't hide treats around the house for later (Dad will find them).

10. Clean your teeth twice before bed.

" I see dead people.*"

The Sixth Sense (1999)

*Spoiler alert!

Before the invention and mass manufacture of plastic-wrapped candy in the 1970s, candy apples — fruit on a stick dipped in red cinnamon syrup — were all the rage at Halloween.

Candied apples were invented accidentally in 1908 by William W. Kolb, a candymaker in New Jersey. As an experiment, Kolb dipped an apple on a stick to use as decoration to entice passers-by into his shop. The apples sold better than the candy as customers presumed they tasted as good as they looked.

They remained popular Halloween treats until the 1970s.

TRICK-OR-TREAT

WORLDWIDE

1. "Dolcetto o scherzetto" – **Italian**
2. "Süßes oder Saures" – **German**
3. "Karkki vai kepponen" – **Finnish**
4. "Truco o trato" – **Spanish**
5. "Bus eller godis" – **Swedish**
6. "Grikk eða gott" – **Icelandic**
7. "Knask eller knep" – **Norwegian**
8. "Doçura ou travessura" – **Portugal**
9. "Avaritiam aut facies" – **Latin**
10. "Ne dati ori nu ne dati"– **Croatian**

TOP 10
HAUNTED NATIONS

According to the Paranormal Activity Index, which tallies UFO sightings with ghost stories, haunted house locations, mythical creatures, and other devilishly despicable data, these 10 countries are the very best when it comes to scare-fests.

1. USA
2. UK
3. Ireland
4. Japan
5. Germany

6. Puerto Rico
7. Philippines
8. Portugal
9. Netherlands
10. Colombia

OH MY GOURD!

According to the Guinness World Records, the heaviest pumpkin record was smashed in 2021, when Stefano Cutrupi, from Italy, grew a horrifying 1,226kg (2,702lb 13.9oz) pumpkin!

That's the same weight as 17 adult men.

One of the most iconic ghost sightings in the UK is Anne Boleyn, the second wife of King Henry VIII and mother of Queen Elizabeth I.

Anne was beheaded at the Tower of London, in May 1536, after being accused of witchcraft. She gave a speech, which ended, **"And thus I take my leave of the world and of you all, and I heartily desire you all to pray for me."**

For centuries, sightings of Anne's headless ghost have roamed the Tower.

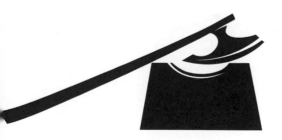

MOST HAUNTED
#2
IRELAND

Ireland is dripping in gooey ectoplasm. According to the *Irish Post*, these old haunts are the best.

1. Wicklow Gaol, Wicklow
("The Gates of Hell"!)

2. Charles Fort, Cork
(The White Lady)

3. The Hellfire Club, Dublin
("Sex, drinking, debauchery and animal torture were all commonplace")

4. Aughrim Battlefield, Galway
(Jacobite Army massacre)

5. Loftus Hall, Wexford
(Annie Tottenham locked herself in a room
never to come out)

6. Glenullin, Derry
(Abhartach, the world's first vampire)

7. Cork District Lunatic Asylum
(Hallaran's torture chair)

8. Abbey of the Black Hag, Limerick
(Countess Desmond was buried alive)

9. Coolbawn House, County Wexford
(electrified servant girl!)

10. Ballinagarde House, Limerick
(a sinister figure on horseback!)

CHAPTER

TWO

WITCHING HOUR

As thriller-aficionado Vincent Price once infamously slow-jammed on Michael Jackson's Halloween hit, "The midnight hour is close at hand/Creatures crawl in search of blood/ To terrorize y'all's neighbourhood."

Yes, the underworld is fit to burst; ghosts are about to come and bust the Witching Hour wide open.

Who ya gonna call?

Six Signs Your House Is Haunted*

1. Creaky stairs (dad's put on weight)

2. Unexplained smells (Dad)

3. Doors open and shut on their own
(uneven walls)

4. Things fall off the wall
(badly hung by Dad)

5. Rooms feel cold (boiler turned off)

6. Electronics turn on by themselves
(dog's sat on remote)

7. Things go missing (in wallet)

8. Whispering voices (when Mum's
got her best friend over)

9. Strange creepy feeling
(when you enter a child's room)

10. Loud bangs and bumps
(when Dad's lost his glasses)

*Or needs repairs and/or cleaning, and/or you have children

According to Guinness World Records, the world's loudest scream belongs to Jill Drake, from the UK.  Her shriek measured 129 decibels, at a Halloween event in London, October 2000. That's equal to the noise a jet makes taking-off!

A SURVEY CONDUCTED BY THE PEW RESEARCH CENTRE CONCLUDED THAT ONE IN FIVE AMERICANS BELIEVE THEY'VE SEEN, OR BEEN IN THE PRESENCE OF, A GHOST.

The Haunted House Association
of the US, which oversees 1,200
spooktacular spaces, is worth more
than $500 million in tourism.

Ancient Egyptians were the first to haunt their own houses.

To ensure tomb raiders kept clear of their treasures (buried with their mummified bodies), they ambushed their pyramid tombs with moving walls, mazes and booby-traps filled with snakes and rats.

66

Kids, it's time we told you the true story and put your fears to rest. It's a story of murder and revenge from beyond the grave. It all started on the thirteenth hour of the thirteenth day of the thirteenth month.
We were there to discuss the misprinted calendars the school had purchased.

99

Marge Simpson
The Simpsons, "Treehouse of Horrors VI"

CANDY LOBBY

In the US, Halloween also means the end of Daylight Savings time. And the two could be connected.

In 2007, the end date for daylight savings was moved a week later to the first Sunday in November. It means that Halloweener's must remember to turn their clocks back after trick-or-treating.

The reason for the move (maybe) was down to the all-powerful interests of the candy lobby, who demanded an extra hour of daylight on Halloween to maximize candy sales as trick-or-treaters could stay out longer.

Centuries ago, in the UK, scratch marks were discovered on the inside of coffins – "dead" people had accidently been buried alive. To stop this from happening, a piece of string attached to a bell was tied around the wrist of corpses. Someone was then hired to sit in the graveyard all night and listen out for the bell. This is where the term "graveyard shift" comes from.

The first printed record
of a word to mean
"Halloween" appeared in
*The Chronicle of the Grey
Friars of London* in 1556,
spelled as
"**HALHALON**".

Among the bonny winding banks,
Where Doon rins, wimplin' clear,
Where Bruce ance ruled the
martial ranks,
And shook his Carrick spear,
Some merry, friendly, country-folks,
Together did convene,
To burn their nits, and pou their stocks,
And haud their Halloween
Fu' blithe that night.

Robert Burns,
"Halloween" (stanza two of 28), 1786*

*One of the first recorded writings on Halloween

The word "**Halloween**" can be traced back to 1745.

It is derived from the Scottish term for All Hallows' Eve (the evening before All Hallows' Day), or "Saints' evening". In Scots, the word evening was contracted to e'en or een.

Over time, All Hallows Eve became Halloween.

GUISING, SOULING AND MUMMING

Before it became a globally revered
phenomenon known as trick-or-treating, the
Scottish had invented guising (also called
souling and mumming) – children disguised
in costume going from door to door asking
for food or coins on All Hallows' Eve as far
back as the mid-1500s.

GIVE THEM NIGHTMARES

The esteemed and beloved children's scare master, Neil Gaiman, recommends his favourite terrible tales that guarantee to ensure your children are afraid of the dark forever (in a good way).

1. *The Time of the Ghost*
by Diana Wynne Jones

2. *The Eyes of the Dragon*
by Stephen King

3. *The Halloween Tree*
by Ray Bradbury

4. *The House With a Clock in Its Walls* by John Bellairs

5. *Scary Stories to Tell in the Dark* by Alvin Schwartz

6. *Goosebumps* by R.L. Stine

7. *The Witches* by Roald Dahl

8. *Krabat (AKA the Satanic Mill)* by Ottfried Preussler

9. *The Thief of Always* by Clive Barker

10. *Something Wicked Comes This Way* by Ray Bradbury

The origins of Halloween belong completely to the Scottish, and their ancient Celtic pagan tradition called Samhain. Pronounced saw-win, Samhain celebrates the moment summer turns to autumn, roughly at the end of October.

For Celts, New Year began on November 1st, so the day before they celebrated All Hallows' Eve, a day marked by diminishing light and orange leaves, a day they believed the boundaries between the world of the living and the dead merged.

" On Halloween you get to become anything that you want to be. "

Ava Dellaira

" Every day is Halloween, isn't it? For some of us. "

Tim Burton

66
One of the
secrets of a happy
life is continuous
small treats. **99**

Iris Murdoch

66

A witch never gets caught. Don't forget that she has magic in her fingers and devilry dancing in her blood.

99

Roald Dahl,
The Witches

TOP 10

HORROR-MAD NATIONS IN THE WORLD

Based on their Halloween costume search history in October.

1. USA
2. UK
3. Mexico
4. Brazil
5. Germany

6. Turkey
7. Australia
8. Canada
9. Columbia
10. Russia

THE HAUNTED SUMMER

In April 1815, the most powerful volcanic eruption in human history was recorded at Mount Tambora, Indonesia. Ash scattered around the world, obscured the sun and lowered global temperatures. Those 12 months were known as the Year With No Summer.

On June 16, 1816, authors Percy Shelley, Mary Wollstonecraft (later Shelley), Lord Byron and John Polidori gathered at the Villa Diodati, Geneva. Inspired by the bleak year without sunshine, and lightning and thunder at the window, Byron devised a "ghost story competition". That weekend, Polidori wrote the first treatment for the world's first vampire novel, *The Vampyre,* and Wollstonecraft wrote *Frankenstein*. The horror genre was born.

The first written mention of
"Jack O Lantern's" in America
appeared in Nathaniel Hawthorne's
1835 story, *The Great Carbuncle*,
about a gang of adventurers who
find a magic stone.

**"Hide it under thy cloak,
say'st thou?
Why, it will gleam through
the holes, and make thee look
like a jack-o'-lantern".**

Martin Luther, he of Lutheran domination (named after him, obvs), chose All Hallows' Eve in 1517 to start the Protestant Reformation. Luther knew that many people would attend church in Wittenberg, Germany, that Hallowmas evening and see his *Ninety-Five Theses*, a document that divided the Catholic Church, nailed to the church's door. The ballsy move kickstarted the Protestant split of the Church.

66

Don't be afraid of being scared. To be afraid is a sign of common sense. Only complete idiots are not afraid of anything.

99

Carlos Ruiz Zafón

"I AM THE MONSTER THAT BREATHING MEN WOULD KILL... I AM DRACULA"

Bram Stoker
Dracula (1897)

There is a child in every one of us who is still a trick-or-treater looking for a brightly-lit front porch.

Robert Brault

65

SPOOKY SHAKESPEARE

William Shakespeare loved ghost stories, witches, the macabre and anything to do with "All-hallond eve" (as he called it in *Measure to Measure*, in 1604).
Here's the Bard's spookiest lines:

"The graves stood tenantless, and the sheeted dead
Did squeak and gibber in the Roman streets."

Hamlet

"Now it is the time of night
That the graves, all gaping wide,
Every one lets forth his sprite
In the church-way paths to glide."

A Midsummer Night's Dream

"Eye of newt, and toe of frog, Wool of bat, and tongue of dog, Adder's fork, and blind-worm's sting, Lizard's leg, and owlet's wing, For a charm of powerful trouble, Like a hell-broth boil and bubble."

Macbeth

"Tis now the very witching time of night, when churchyards yawn and hell itself breathes out Contagion to this world."

Hamlet

"Hell is empty and all the devils are here."

The Tempest

"By the pricking of my thumbs, something wicked this way comes."

Macbeth

THE VERB "SCARE" DATES BACK TO 1200, AND DERIVES FROM THE OLD NORSE WORD SKIRRA.

"
Monsters are real, ghosts are real too. They live inside us, and sometimes, they win.

"

Stephen King,
The Shining (1977)

In 1727, Janet Horne became the last person to be executed legally for witchcraft in the UK.

Contrary to popular belief, no witches were burnt at the stake during the Salem, Massachusetts Witch Trial, 1692–1693.

More than 200 people were accused of witchcraft, thirty were found guilty, and nineteen were executed by hanging.

11%

According to *USA Today*, it is estimated that 11 per cent of the US population is afraid of the dark.

64%

IN THE UK,
ACCORDING TO THE
MIRROR, 64 PER
CENT OF ADULTS
ADMIT THEY ARE
STILL SCARED OF
THE DARK.

73

"

WE MAKE UP HORRORS TO HELP US COPE WITH THE REAL ONES

"

Stephen King

"

*WHERE THERE
IS NO IMAGINATION
THERE IS NO
HORROR*

"

Arthur Conan Doyle

75

One in five Britons regularly check under the bed for monsters and close the cupboard and wardrobe doors before getting into bed. The same ones also confessed they do not like to have a foot hanging out from underneath the covers in case "something grabs it".

The most common time for adults to become scared of the dark is 2:30am - the start of the "Witching Hour" (often considered to be between 3am and 4am).*

* Did you know that Jesus Christ supposedly died at 3pm? The "Devil's Hour" is believed to be at 3am as an inversion of this time.

One in five people are really, really scared of bats.*

* Five out of five bats are scared of humans.**

** If you're still scared, stock up on cinnamon,
eucalyptus, cloves, mint and peppermint.
Bats are scared of those smells.

WICCAPHOBIA

The fear of witches.

Here Comes the

When humans get scared – watching a super-scary movie, for example – they experience a rush of the hormone, adrenaline, and a release of several endorphins: dopamine, serotonin and oxytocin. These "feel good" biochemicals flood our senses with a feeling of euphoria.

As brains are immediately able to perceive a sense of safety in your own living room, or cinema, the fear you feel is quickly diminished, leaving viewers pumped with a sense of satisfaction.

66
This is my costume. I'm a homicidal maniac. They look just like everyone else.
99

Wednesday
The Addams Family (1991)

" Nothing on earth is so beautiful as the final haul on Halloween night. "

Steve Almond

HORROR

PLAYLIST#2

CLASSICS

1. "Monster Mash" – **Bobby Pickett**

2. "Thriller" – **Michael Jackson feat. Vincent Price**

3. "(Don't Fear) The Reaper" – **Blue Oyster Cult**

4. "Feed My Frankenstein" – **Alice Cooper**

5. "Season of the Witch" – **Lana del Ray**

6. "I Put A Spell On You" – **Screamin' Jay Hawkins**

7. "Ghostbusters" – **Ray Parker Jnr.**

8. "The Phantom of the Opera Overture" – **Andrew Lloyd Webber**

9. "Superstition" – **Stevie Wonder**

10. "Time Warp" – ***Rocky Horror Show* cast**

66

It's as much fun to scare as to be scared.

99

Vincent Price

25%

In 2021, a quarter of costumes worn on Halloween were based on popular characters from TV shows or movies.

Approximately 50 per cent kept it simple and either reused a costume, or spooked-up a sweater already owned.

CHAPTER

THREE

LITTLE HORRORS

From its earliest origins to its hideously disfigured monstrous modern mutation, trick-or-treating and Halloween is now the most fun a family can have together without killing each other.

Jog on, Christmas. Beat it, Easter.
Take a walk, Thanksgiving.
A new overlord is here to slay.
All hail, Halloween!

" NEVER TRUST THE LIVING. "

Beetlejuice
Beetlejuice (1988)

It is widely believed that when 6 million Irish fled to the US in the 1850s to escape the potato famine, they took their Halloween traditions with them, leading to a boom in the festival's popularity nationwide.

In 1874, French composer Camille Saint-Saëns wrote perhaps the first pieces of music written specifically for Halloween.

Called "Danse Macabre", the musical-poem tells the story of the Grim Reaper waking at midnight to host a Halloween dance with skeletons.

The Celts invented
Halloween 2,000 years ago.
When the Romans invaded
(between 43 AD and 84
AD), they merged their late
summer festivals,

Feralia, which honoured the
dead, and their celebration
of Pomona, the goddess
of harvest, with the Celts,
Samhain traditions.

66

Anyone could see that the wind was a special wind this night, and the darkness took on a special feel because it was All Hallows' Eve.

99

Ray Bradbury
The Halloween Tree (1972)

66

The farther we've gotten from the magic and mystery of our past, the more we've come to need Halloween.

99

Paula Curan

HORROR

PLAYLIST#3

MONSTERS AND DEMONDS

1. **"Wolves"** – Selena Gomez

2. **"I'm in Love with a Monster"** – Fifth Harmony

3. **"Zombie"**– Cranberries

4. **"Monster"** – Lady Gaga

5. **"Haunted"** – Beyoncé

6. **"She Wolf"** – Shakira

7. **"Scary Monsters and Super Creeps"** – David Bowie

8. **"Witchy Woman"** – The Eagles

9. **"Sympathy for the Devil"** – Rolling Stones

10. **"Black Magic Woman"** – Fleetwood Mac

66

I've seen enough horror movies to know that any weirdo wearing a mask is never friendly.

99

Elizabeth,
Friday the 13th Part VI: Jason Lives (1986)

In 609 AD,
Pope Boniface IV
established the Catholic
feast of All Hallows' Day
on May 13. A few decades
later, Pope Gregory III
moved All Hallows' Day
to November 1 so that
it replaced the Celts'
traditions with a more
church-heavy influence.

It was in the 1300s that the Aztecs began celebrating "Día de Los Muertos" - the Day of the Dead, a Mexican equivalent of the Celts' traditions of honouring the dead before winter.

On Día de Los Muertos, Mexican children trick-or-treat by asking "¿Me da mi calaverita?", which translates to "Can you give me my little skull?"

In the 1800s, as ghost stories began to litter literature (see **The Haunted Summer**, page 60) ghosts stopped being depicted as translucent apparitions, and began to be characterized as souls wearing burial shrouds, namely bedsheets.

Up until the 1970s, Halloween costumes were scary but not horrifying.

That changed in 1978 with the release of the first

HALLOWEEN

movie in which the serial slasher Michael Myers wears a pale William Shatner face mask as he murders for revenge.

Trick-or-treating effectively stopped during World War II due to sugar rationing.

Once rationing was lifted in June 1947, candy companies ramped up commercial production greater than ever before to meet the overwhelming demand.

Within five years, trick-or-treating for candy was commonplace.

In the US, Halloween face masks and paper costumes began appearing in the 1920s.

A soul! a soul! a soul-cake!
Please good Missis, a soul-cake!
An apple, a pear, a plum, or a cherry,
Any good thing to make us all merry.
One for Peter, two for Paul
Three for Him who made us all.

(Nineteenth century souling song)

* Soul cakes, small round cakes made with nutmeg,
ginger, cinnamon, and raisins, were popular
Halloween treats. The cakes were marked with
a cross, representing a soul being freed from
purgatory when the cake was devoured.

GRAVEYARD SMASH

"Monster Mash" by Boris Pickett is one of the few "graveyard smashes" to have hit the top spot in the charts.

In 1962, "Monster Mash" became, and remained, the best soundtrack to trick-or-treating.

It was banned by the BBC, until it was re-released in 1973, for being "too morbid".

During Samhain,
Celts would set
a place and leave
food at the table
for deceased family
members who
would return from
the dead for one
night only.

"

Production designer Tommy Lee Wallace came in with a clown mask he had bought from a magic shop on, and we went, 'Ooh, that's kind of scary.' Then he put on a William Shatner mask, and we stopped dead and said, 'It's perfect.' They spray-painted it white, cut the eye holes bigger, and the rest is spine-tingling history.

"

Nick Castle
on the origin of the original
Halloween face mask

The legendary magician and illusionist and Harry Houdini died on Halloween in 1926, following a ruptured appendix. Before his death, Houdini and his wife, Bess, devised a message that he would use during a séance so she would know if he had crossed over to the spirit world. The message was,

"Rosabelle–answer–tell–pray–answer–look–tell–answer–answer–tell".

Bess gave up after 10 years.

ONE QUARTER OF ALL THE CANDY SOLD IN THE US EACH YEAR IS PURCHASED FOR HALLOWEEN.

Some people (not arachnophobes) believe if you see a spider on Halloween, it means a deceased loved one is watching over you.

109

60%

of children prefer to receive chocolate treats on Halloween.

According to some, if you walk backwards on Halloween, with your clothes inside-out, you are guaranteed to see a witch at midnight.

Try it out...

It is believed that if a child is born on Halloween, they will be able to talk to the spirits.

Vanilla Ice was born on Halloween.

Just sayin'.

According to the
Daily Mail, an average
calorie haul from an
evening of trick-or-
treating in the US will be
around

4,800 calories.

That's three cups of sugar.
This would take two
straight days of energetic
exercise to burn off.

The Irish word

SAMHAIN

translates to
"summer's end".

The name Jack-o'-lantern first originated from an Irish folktale about a man named Stingy Jack who tricked the Devil repeatedly into keeping his life.

When Jack died, the Devil forced him to walk the earth for eternity carrying a carved-out turnip with a burning coal in it to help light his way.

TOP 10

TRICK-OR-TREAT CANDIES

In a 2021 candystore.com survey, these candies are the US's best*, in terms of popularity.

1. Reese's Cups (Candy corn)
2. M&M's (Circus Peanuts)
3. Skittles (Peanut Butter Kisses)
4. Snickers (Smarties)
5. Sour Patch Kids (Necco wafers)
6. Kit Kat (Wax Coke bottles)
7. Twix (Mary Janes)
8. Hershey Bar (Tootsie Rolls)
9. Butterfinger (Good & Plenty)
10. Nerds (Black liquorice)

* (The worst)

During
Samhain,
Celtic people
would wear animal heads
and skins in order to
scare away ghosts.

100%

of parents stash Halloween candy to enjoy later in the year.

(Only 50 per cent admitted to it.)

15 MILLION
PUMPKINS ARE GROWN IN THE UK EACH YEAR.

Ever wondered why a large fire is called a bonfire? It originated from the phrase "bone fire", a practice started during Samhain, when cattle bones would be thrown onto a fire.

Remember:

Chocolate can be frozen in the freezer and remains good to eat for up to three months past its expiration date.

FUN SIZE

The world's largest chocolate manufacturer, Mars, started producijng mini chocolate bars in 1961 so they could specifically target trick-or-treaters.

It was Mars who coined the phrase "fun size" in 1968. The first fun size bars were Snickers and Milky Way.

When rival chocolatiers, and makers of Baby Ruth and Butterfinger bars, began making fun size bars, Mars sued them… and lost. Thankfully. Now every chocolate maker is free to make fun.

According to National Retail Federation, in 2021, 1.8 million children dressed as

SPIDERMAN

in the US, more than any other superhero.

1.6 million dressed as their favourite princess and, yes, princesses are superheroes.

Things Parents Say On Halloween

1. "I think you've had enough."
2. "That's enough."

3. "Last house of the night."

4. "OK, this is really the last house tonight."

5. "Your teeth will fall out if you eat any more."

6. "Someone's had a bit too much sugar."

7. "So-and-so makes a very sexy witch."

8. "Can you wait until we get home to have a wee?"

9. "Is it bedtime yet?"

10. "Can I have one of your treats?"

47%

of Britons believe
that ghosts are real.

CHAPTER

FOUR

SMASHING PUMPKINS

Pumpkins, bats, cats, owls, witches, vampires, monsters, demons, ghosts, chocolate, candy – Halloween is a loosely defined feast of all things frightening and zeitgeisty. Superheroes? Sure. Sexy witches? Whatever. Pirates? Knock yourself out. Halloween is whatever you want it to be.

The first citywide Halloween celebration in the US occurred in Anoka, Minnesota, in 1921.

72%

of U.S. parents admit
to stealing their children's
Halloween candy.

"

A mask tells us more than a face.

"

Oscar Wilde

"

Halloween was confusing.
All my life my parents said,
'Never take candy from
strangers.' And then they
dressed me up and said,
'Go beg for it.'

"

Rita Rudner

TOP 10

HORROR MOVIES OF ALL TIME

(by global box office)

1. It (2017) $701,083,042

2. I Am Legend (2007) $585,532,684

3. Jaws (1975) $470,700,000

4. It: Chapter Two (2019) $469,566,806

5. The Exorcist (1973) $428,214,478

6. The Nun (2018) $363,391,647

7. Hannibal (2001) $350,100,280

8. A Quiet Place (2018) $334,876,670

9. The Conjuring (2013) $317,744,402

10. Resident Evil: $314,101,190
    The Final Chapter (2016)

"
If we went to a
Halloween party dressed
as Batman and Robin,
I'd go as Robin. That's how
much you mean to me. **"**

Chazz
Blades of Glory (2007)

"

When we're together, darling, every night is Halloween.

"

Morticia Addams
The Addams Family (1964)

"

Halloween is Christmas for jerks.

"

Amy
Brooklyn Nine-Nine, Season 1,
Episode 6: "Halloween"

"

Halloween is the sequel to
Halloween, but not the sequel to
Halloween. Technically it's
Halloween 2 but ignores the events
of *Halloween* 2 and *Halloween* 2.
It's the first *Halloween* film to bring
back Jamie Lee Curtis, except for
Halloween 2, *Halloween* 7 and
Halloween 8. But finally the series
has brought back John Carpenter
in some capacity for the first time,
except for *Halloween* 2 and
Halloween 3. It's also the first

Halloween film to ignore the previous films in the franchise's timeline, except for *Halloween* 3, *Halloween* 4 which ignores *Halloween* 3, *Halloween* 7, which ignores *Halloween* 3, *Halloween* 4, *Halloween* 5, and *Halloween* 6. But aside from all that, it's a totally fresh and new start for the *Halloween* franchise!

"

Jay
Half in the Bag, Season 8, Episode 19:
"Halloween"

MOST HAUNTED
#3
UK

Wanderlust's poll of the UK's most horrible places (for ghosts) is pretty spot on.

1. Pendle Hill, Lancashire
(witches!)

2. Tower of London
(headless Anne Boleyn!)

3. Ancient Ram Inn
(incubus!)

4. Berry Pomeroy Castle, Devon
(The Blue Lady)

5. Plas Mawr, Wales
(dead Dr Dick!)

6. Blicklling Hall, Norfolk
(Falstaff!)

7. Dunster Castle, Somerset
(disembodied feet!)

8. Springhill House, Ireland
(sad wife!)

9. Ham House, Richmond
(husband poisoner!)

10. Treasurer's House, York
(dead soldiers!)

GHOSTWATCH

On Halloween 1992, the BBC infamously aired *Ghostwatch*, a "live" haunting of a real family home in north-west London. It was watched by 11 million people – many of whom believed it to be too real to be fake.

By the end of the show, viewers (many of whom were children) were left traumatized and with PTSD, adamant the BBC had raised demonic forces from the underworld and broadcast it to the world.

HUMANS ARE BORN WITH TWO FEARS: THE FEAR OF FALLING, AND THE FEAR OF LOUD NOISES.

THE REST WE CREATE IN OUR MINDS.

Movies Set at Halloween That Aren't

HALLOWEEN

1. Poltergeist
2. The Return of Dracula
3. Sleepy Hollow
4. Silence of the Lambs
5. Pet Sematary
6. Nightmare on Elm Street
7. The Exorcist
8. Donnie Darko
9. Scream
10. The Blair Witch Project

Dare to be the tricked this Halloween.
Offer the local trick-or-treaters the unpopular alternative to candy.

1. Glow-in-the-dark vampire teeth
2. Hair scrunchies
3. Slime pots
4. Fridge magnets
5. Bubble tubs
6. Glow sticks
7. Plastic spiders
8. Whoopie cushions
9. Snap bracelets
10. Pencil toppers

The majority of children outgrow the fear of the dark by ages 4 to 5.

One in five children will remain fearful of the dark for the rest of their lives.

144

FOR THE FIRST TIME IN HISTORY, IN 2021, AMERICANS SPENT MORE THAN $10 BILLION ON HALLOWEEN.

THE MOST BLACK BLACK IS CALLED VANTABLACK. IT'S BEYOND BLACK. IT'S TERRIFYING.

According to *The Sun*,
an estimated
20 MILLION
people in
the US have a phobia
of Friday the 13th.

Only 12 out of the 40,000 spider species on earth can cause death in adult humans.

In the UK, in 2021, more than 30 million people dressed up for Halloween.

The next day, 7 million costumes were thrown away – that's the equivalent of 83 million plastic bottles of waste.

1 in 10

**Americans
refuse to celebrate
Halloween.**

"

I was the only child on my block on Halloween to go, 'Trick or trout!'...
'Here comes that young Williams boy again. Better get some fish.'

"

Robin Williams

SMASHING PUMPKINS

THE WAR OF THE WORLDS

On Mischief Night, 1938, soon-to-be famous filmmaker Orson Welles narrated an adaptation of H. G. Wells' novel *The War of the Worlds* broadcast live on radio in America for a special Halloween episode that began at 8 pm. Welles converted the novel into fake news bulletins describing a Martian invasion of New Jersey.

At home, audiences believed the invasion to be real, inducing mass panic among listeners. "If I'd planned to wreck my career," Welles said after, "I couldn't have gone about it better."

"

When my kids were younger, and they'd go trick-or-treating, and I would go with them, I'd wear the *Halloween* mask. If people didn't give them candy, I'd take off the mask, and blow a kiss.

"

William Shatner
The face of the iconic *Halloween* mask

HORRIFYING PHOBIAS

#1

Achluophobia	fear of darkness
Ailurophobia	fear of cats
Arachnophobia	fear of spiders
Chiroptophobia	fear of bats
Coimetrophobia	fear of cemeteries
Coulrophobia	fear of clowns
Chrysophobia	fear of the colour orange
Hexakosioihexek- ontahexaphobia	fear of the number 666
Oneirophobia	fear of dreams

13

The origin of the unlucky nature of this number is said to have originated in Norse mythology when the trickster god, and popular Halloween costume for males aged 18–35, Loki, was the thirteenth guest at a party he was not invited to. There, Loki caused chaos, ordering his brother Höðr to shoot his other brother, Balder, with a mistletoe-tipped arrow. Cheeky.

On October 31, 1940, during World War II, the Royal Navy's air force successfully fought off a large-scale German invasion from Luftwaffe aircraft, now known as the Battle of Britain. If the UK had lost, the War could have become very horrifying indeed.

HOLLYWOOD HALLOWEEN

66

Acting is like a Halloween mask that you put on.

99

River Phoenix

Without a doubt, one of the most infamous deaths on Halloween – River Phoenix. The actor died at the age of 23 in 1993, outside a famous Hollywood club, called the Viper Room, after consuming too many drugs. "I was at this Halloween party, and he passed me. He was beyond pale – he looked white. Before I got a chance to say hello, he was gone, driving off to the Viper Room," Leonardo DiCaprio said of Phoenix's death.

CHAPTER
FIVE

TERROR VISION

From horror movies to haunted houses, monsters to murderers, slashers to stick-on gashes, trick-and-treating is the only time of the year when you can scare the ones you hold dear with fear. (Imagine dressing as a pirate for Christmas Day – you'd feel ridiculous, right?) So, enjoy the fun of the fear tonight because tomorrow it'll be back to the terrors of real life.

ON AVERAGE, THERE IS A FRIDAY THE 13TH ONCE EVERY 212.35 DAYS.

Scare your children on Halloween by pretending you are haunted by a really talkative ghost. And if they don't behave, the ghost will just keep on talking. It works.

MOST HAUNTED

#4

CANADA

According to Culture Trip, these are the creepiest caverns in Canada.

1. Craigdarroch Castle, Victoria
(keep eyes peeled for the Woman in the White Dress)

3. Fairmont Banff Springs
(the Bride who fell to her death haunts the stairs)

4. Keg Mansion, Toronto
(the maid who hangs by her neck!)

5. Hi-Ottawa Jail Hostel
(haunted by a Bible-clutching inmate!)

6. Plains of Abraham, Quebec City
(haunted by dead soldiers)

7. Fairmount Empress, Vancouver Island
(Sir Francis Rattenbury walks the halls)

8. Tranquille Sanatorium, Kamloops
(haunted by dead patients)

9. West Point Lighthouse, O'Leary
(Willie, the first lightkeeper, haunts the dark)

10. Baie des Chaleurs Phantom Ship, New Brunswick
(a murdered sailor wants revenge!)

Michael Myers' Movies

Admit it, you've always wanted to know the Halloween franchise, by order of box office success:

1. *Halloween* (2018)

2. *Halloween Kills* (2021)

3. *Halloween* (2007)

4. *Halloween H20: 20 Years Later* (1998)

5. *Halloween* (1978)

6. *Halloween II* (2009)

7. *Halloween: Resurrection* (2002)

8. *Halloween II* (1981)

9. *Halloween 4: The Return of Michael Myers* (1988)

10. *Halloween: The Curse of Michael Myers* (1995)

11. *Halloween III: Season of the Witch* (1982)

12. *Halloween: The Revenge of Michael Myers* (1989)

** Halloween Ends, *the 13th film of the franchise, is released October 2022*

66

I was once arrested
for indecent exposure
when I removed
a Halloween mask.

99

Alfred Hitchcock Presents (1958)

"
Halloween is about candy and scaring people. But mostly candy.

"

Tommy
WandaVision, Episode 6

In the UK,
Snickers is the
most popular
trick-or-treat
chocolate,
closely followed
by Maltesers.

Canada's Top 10 Trick-or-Treat Candies

According to Halloween Alley, these Halloween candies don't suck for Canucks.

1. Reese's Cups
2. Skittles
3. M&Ms
4. Starburst
5. Snickers
6. Mars
7. Kit Kats
8. Sour Patch Kids
9. Coffee Crisp
10. Hershey Kisses

FIGHT OR FLIGHT

Fear is all in the mind. However, it triggers an intense physical reaction in your body.

Once the fear hits, the amygdala, in the middle of your brain, is activated. This organ sends a message to your nervous system, instantly increasing your blood pressure, heart rate and breathing. Your blood rapidly flows away from your heart and into your limbs.

This is your body going into "fight or flight" mode – the more blood in your limbs makes it easier for you to fight, or run for your life.

170

According to Google Trends FrightGeist statistics, these were the most popular Halloween costumes in the US in 2021:

1. Witch
2. Rabbit
3. Dinosaur
4. Spider-Man
5. Cruella de Vil
6. Fairy
7. Harley Quinn
8. Cowboy
9. Clown
10. Chucky
11. Cheerleader
12. Pirate
13. Pumpkin
14. Angel
15. Vampire
16. Among us
17. Zombie
18. 1980s
19. Superhero
20. Devil
21. Joker
22. Ninja
23. Squid Game
24. Doll

171

Pumpkin flesh contains no fat. It's also a great source of potassium and beta-carotene. It also contains minerals including calcium and magnesium, as well as vitamins E, C and B.

Carve your pumpkin into chunks, grate it, and blitz in a blender, and you've got yourself a pumpkin smoothie that's delicious, healthy and zero waste.

"

Halloween quiet? Why, I figured it'd be a big old vamp scare-a-palooza. **"**

Xander
Buffy the Vampire Slayer, Season 2,
Episode 6: "Halloween"

CHAPTER

SIX

HELL RAISERS

The end is nigh! You've survived!
You've made it through the night
without being bludgeoned, or beaten,
slashed or mashed, tortured or torched,
by a chainsaw-wielding serial-killing
psycho, or, even worse, your fructose-
demented children. As the Joker once
famously cackled, "Whatever doesn't kill
you, only makes you stranger."
See you next fear...

BLOODY MARY

"Bloody Mary...Bloody Mary...
Bloody Mary."

Without doubt the most famous first
experience schoolchildren have with ghost
stories is the terrifying tale of Bloody Mary,
the ghost of a woman who murdered her
children many years ago.

According to Halloween folklore, curious
children who want to summon the apparition
for kicks call out her name three times in
front of a mirror.

Dare you to try this at home...go on.

BLOODY MARY RECIPE

Ingredients
– Ice
– 100ml vodka
– 500ml tomato juice
– 1 tbsp lemon juice, plus 2 slices to serve
– Worcestershire sauce
– Tabasco
– pinch of salt
– pinch of black pepper
– 2 celery sticks, to serve

Make it right: Drench the ice in a large jug with the vodka. Add the tomato juice and a dash of lemon juice. Drip in a drop or two of Worcestershire sauce and Tabasco, with a pinch of salt and pepper. Stir until jug is cold. Strain the mix into your glass. Top with fresh ice and dunk a celery stick and slice of lemon. Finally, summon Bloody Mary in front of a mirror as a drinking buddy.

According to the White
House Historical Association,
the first person to decorate
1600 Pennsylvania Avenue
with Halloween
decorations, such as
skeletons,
Jack-o-lanterns,
black cats, owls,
goblins and
disembodied witch
heads, was First Lady
Mamie Eisenhower
in 1958.

There is a full moon
on Halloween every
19 years or so.

Previous years were:
1955, 1974, 2001
and 2020.

It is known as the
Moon's Metonic cycle.*

* The next full moon that lands on a Friday 13.
But that's will be in August 2049.

Today, the word "witch" refers to a flying warts-and-all woman with a broom and lots of black cats. But that's not always been the case. The origin of the word witch comes from an Old English word, wicce, which first meant "wise woman". A gang of witches is a wiccan.

180

HORRIFYING PHOBIAS

#2

Masklophobia	fear of masks and costumes
Melanophobia	fear of the colour black
Necrophobia	fear of death or the dead
Noctiphobia	fear of the night
Nostophobia, ecophobia	fear of returning home
Phasmophobia	fear of ghosts
Taphophobia	fear of graves
Teratophobia	fear of giving birth to a monster
Triskaidekaphobia	fear of the number 13

BART'S PHONE PRANKS

Bart Simpson's famous Halloween phone pranks to poor bar owner Moe Szyslak, in *The Simpsons*, have become the stuff of legend, and became common inspiration Mischief Night pranks for decades.
Here's Bart's best…

1. I.P. Freely

2. Jacques Strap

3. Seymour Butz

4. Mike Rotch

5. Bea O'Problem

6. Anita Bath

7. Maya Buttreeks

8. Haywood U. Cuddleme

9. Ollie Tabooger

10. Drew P. Wiener

Men in the Mask

Halloween would be 73 per cent less scarier if psychos didn't dress in masks. Let's pay tribute to the crazies that make Halloween truly creepy:

1. Michael Myers *(Halloween)*

2. Jason Voorhees *(Friday the 13th)*

3. Pennywise *(It)*

4. Pinhead *(Hellraiser)*

5. Freddy Krueger
(Nightmare on Elm Street)

6. Ghostface *(Scream)*

7. Leatherface *(Texas
Chainsaw Massacre)*

8. Jigsaw *(Saw)*

9. The Rabbit *(Donnie Darko)*

10. God *(The Purge)*

183

According to Less Waste.org,
in 2020, Britons threw away
13 million pumpkins (approximately
half of all that were purchased) after
Halloween.

The same year, in the US, 1 billion lbs
of pumpkins were thrown away.

STOP.

Put your pumpkin to good use:
Pumpkin soup, pumpkin pie,
pumpkin hummus, pumpkin
smoothie, pumpkin pickle, pumpkin
cheesecake, pumpkin cupcakes and
roasted pumpkin.

Five-or-so millennia ago, a
black cat was considered
good luck. Today, they are
witches' BFFs and considered
a curse – especially if
one crosses your path on
Halloween. In Ancient
Egyptian times, the
goddess Bastet
was a black cat, and
harming
a black cat was
punishable by death.

Creature Collective Nouns

As detailed by the rather wonderful *Dignity of Dragons* by Jacqueline Ogburn and Nicoletta Ceccoli, these are the imaginative collective nouns of Halloween beasties, and real animals.

MYTH	REAL
A stumble of zombies	A murder of crows
A coffin of vampires	A leash of foxes
A howling of werewolves	A bloat of hippopotami
A bolt of Frankensteins	A cackle of hyenas
A tanna of mummies	A clutter of spiders
A caldron of witches	A shadow of jaguars
A clang hunchbacks	A smack of jellyfish
An ectoplasm of phantoms	A pandemonium of parrots
A haunting of ghosts	A parliament of owls
A decapitation of headless horsemen	An unkindness of ravens
A tinker of gremlins	A crash of rhinoceroses
A hunger of ghouls	A shiver of sharks
A husk of scarecrows	A stench of skunks
A marrow of skeletons	A knot of toads
A scream of victims	A fever of stingrays

TREATS BY DECADE

According to the Daily Meal, these are the top 10
trick-or-treat candies in the U.S. by decade.

1920s: Baby Ruth

1930s: Three Musketeers

1940s: M&Ms

1950s: Atomic Fireballs
(15 million are eaten every week!)

1960s: SweetTarts

1970s: Laffy Taffy

1980s: Skittles

1990s: Airheads

2000s: Nerds Rope

2010s: Reese's Peanut Butter Cups

2020s: Reese's Peanut Butter Cups

TWO BILLION DOLLARS' WORTH OF AMERICA AND CANADA'S MOST POPULAR TRICK-OR-TREAT CANDY, REESE'S PEANUT BUTTER CUPS, ARE SOLD EVERY YEAR.

MISCHIEF NIGHT

For those who love a trick as well as a treat, don't worry, October 30, has got your back. It's Mischief Night. Local children of all ages are semi-encouraged to vandalize the neighbourhood with good-natured pranks.

Usual lampooning includes: toilet papering trees and houses, "doorbell ditching" (ringing and running), egging houses and people, setting off fireworks in bins, and dialling random phone numbers and asking to speak to "Hugh Jass", and ilk.

DEINDIVIDUATION

Scarier than any psycho in a mask is the concept of deindividuation. This term describes what happens when a group of children are together wearing masks. They are vastly more likely to be horrible.

A recent Halloween Study showed that masked children who were by themselves stole 14 per cent more trick-or-treat candy when compared to those who could be identified. A group of masked children also stole more than twice as much (36 per cent) candy as those without masks.

Australia - which is at the height of spring, not autumn, during Halloween - now enjoys Halloween as much as the rest of the world.

In the past five years, Halloween decoration sales have soared by 82 per cent, and costume sales have increased by 31 per cent.

"

Halloween is in your hearts. Every time a little kid cries in fear, that's Halloween. Every time something repulsive ends up in a mailbox, that is Halloween. As long as you carry the spirit of destruction and vandalism in your hearts, every day is Halloween.

"

Francis
Malcolm in the Middle, Season 2, Episode 2:
"Halloween Approximately"